Object Lessons

pendergrast

OBject Lessons

A Book o' Drawin's

by:

← James T.

 Vintage Books   **A Division of Random House**   **New York**

A Vintage Original, June 1988
First Edition

Copyright © 1988 by James T. Pendergrast

Library of Congress Cataloging-in-Publication Data
Pendergrast, James T.
Object lessons.
"A Vintage original."
1. American wit and humor, Pictorial.
I. Title.
NC1429.P396A4   1988   741.5'973   87-45930
ISBN 0-394-75755-6 (pbk.)

Author photo copyright © 1987 by Deborah Feingold

Manufactured in the United States of America
10   9   8   7   6   5   4   3   2   1

To my nephews,
Neil and Trevor

Thanks to everyone who has given me a hand, like, for example,
Theron Raines, Marilyn Abraham, Mike Waldman, and others,
and thanks most specially to David Rosenthal,
Derek Ungless, and Jann Wenner.
Also the members of the Academy (of Beaux Arts),
without whom none of this would have been necessary.

Introduction:
Hope you like these drawings.
—James T. Pendergrast

contents ↘

↖ table

P

I. The Importance of Defining Your Terms

Nown

← Typo

The Importance of defining your terms

Whatchamacallit

Gizmo

pendergrast

3

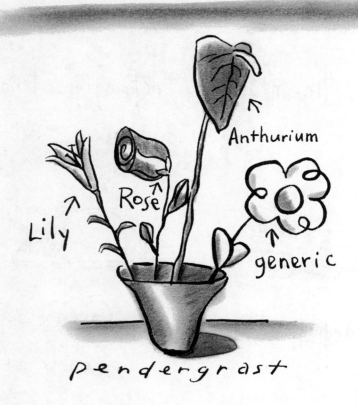

Lily

Rose

Anthurium

generic

pendergrast

4

the Importance of Defining Your Terms

Step on a Crack
Break your Mother's <u>Back</u>

Step on a <u>Line</u>
Break your Mother's
<u>Spine</u>

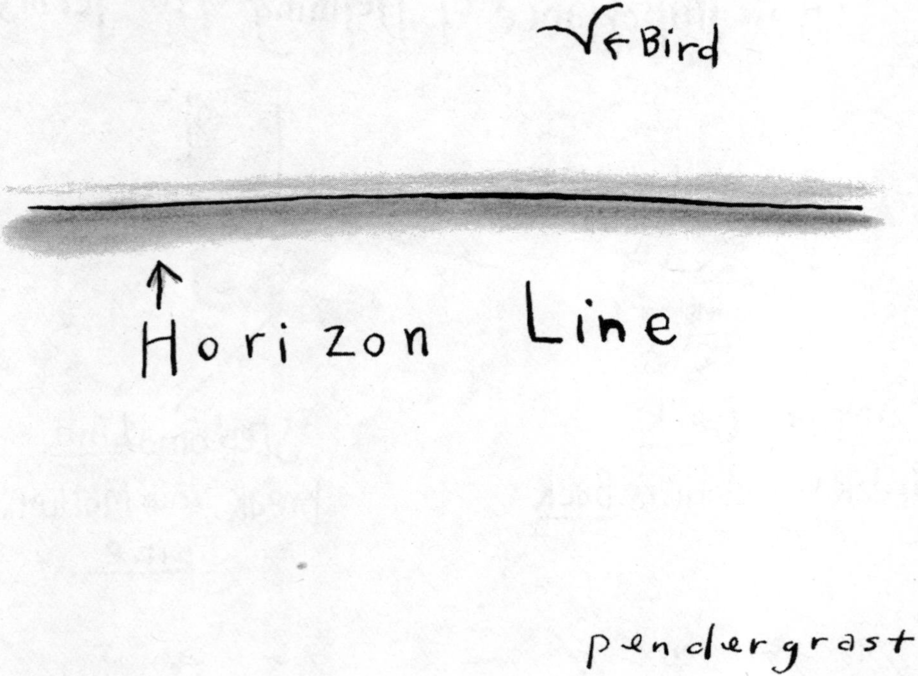

√ ← Bird

Horizon Line

↑

pendergrast

 Analog

 Digital

 generic

 etc.

7

The Importance of Defining Your Terms

Mouse

Whatsit

pendergrast

the Importance of Defining Your Terms

Bouquet   Odor

pendergrast

9

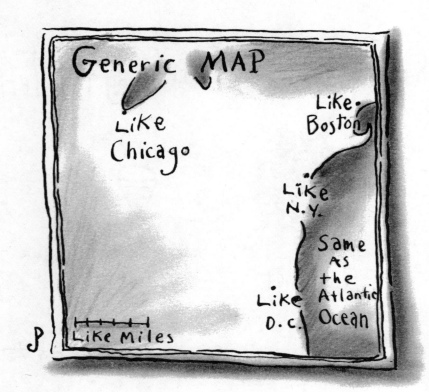

The Importance of Defining Your Terms

Doughnut   Thing-a-ma-bob

pendergast

COLOR

SLEEPING DOG

pendergast

12

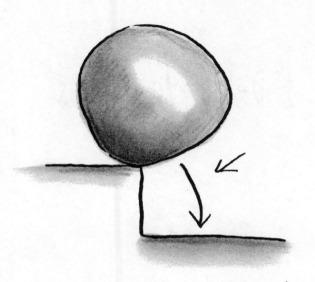

pendergrast

* etc.

13

The Importance of Defining Your Terms

Hologram

Candygram

14

Shake

Rattle

Roll

pendergrast

15

The Importance of Defining Your Terms

Poet standing on a cliff contemplating the vagaries of life

Bowling Ball

16

pendergrast

STAR

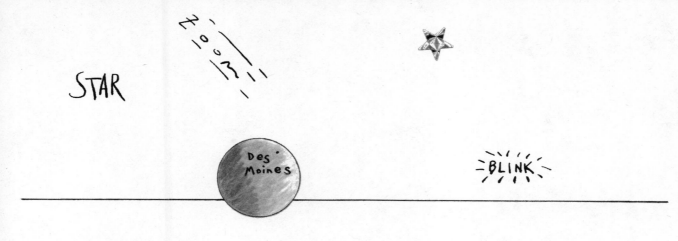

Des Moines

BLINK

ASTRONOMICAL DEALS 'N' WHATSITS

P

17

2. NATURAL HISTORY

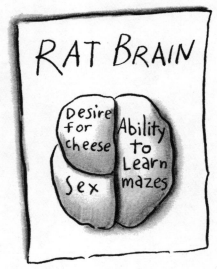

RAT BRAIN

Desire for cheese

Ability to Learn mazes

Sex

P

"OK, if this is purely instinctive behavior, why do they taste so damn good?"

pendergrast

21

The Dead End Kits

"You shoulda been there, Larry—these babes were wearin' reflecto flea collars"

"wow"

pendergrast

23

24 pendergrast

25

A Waterbug Has A Transforming Experience

"wow"

26

pendergrast

A waterbug steps in Cat Barf

DAMN!

pendergrast

Shark Water Ballet

pendergrast

pendergrast

30

* etc.

Fish asking himself the famous
question: "Why is there air?"

pendergrast

BIG TYRANNOSAURUS ON CAMPUS

So I said, "Listen, Charlie, I ain't stickin' my ass in no mouse trap just to satisfy some creepy bondage fantasies you got." Can you imagine the nerve of that guy?

pendergrast

34

3. the Iron City

Insert
RearEnd
Here
←

NYC
vise
Co.

𝒫

HeadQuarters For the Evil Roach Empire!

pendergast   37

1) N. Y. C.

38

pendergrast

40

The Haunted Apt. Bldg.

← pot
roast
odor

pendergast

41

N.Y. Commemoratives

| Empire State Bldg. | Chrysler Bldg. | Statue of Liberty | World Trade Center |
| Central Park | U.N. | Battery Park | Staten Island Ferry |

pendergast

New Yorker's Birthright

CROWDER'S LICENSE

(signature)

Has official permission to get in line in front of anybody Else

pendergrast

A Common Sight

pendergrast

46

CabBie's Handbook

Public Service

CAB

BABY
A BOARD

I'D Like to whack your BABY with A BOARD

(detail)

Pendergrast

47

pendergrast

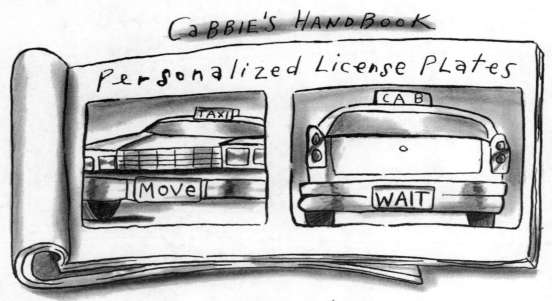

50

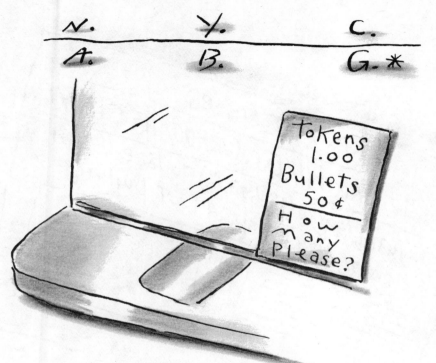

* After Bernie Goetz

pendergrast

NY Times

NEW YORK HIRES SURROGATE CITY!

Tijuana, Mexico ("Baby TJ") to take Leona Helmsley, Don Trump, AT&T Building

New Addition to Tijuana skyline

52

P endergrast

Great Inventions of N.Y.C.

BIG POWWOW Tonight

the "CABBIE Hole" Anti-Spill Device

JAVA

the Doorman

pendergrast

53

4. Travel

P

p end ergr ast

57

58   p   en   der   gra   st

When in France...

Le pop tart

La Surrealisme

L'Amour...

Le Big Ben

L'ice cream
Sandwich

Le Bozo

Idle Thoughts

Rm Bm Bm Bm

Then

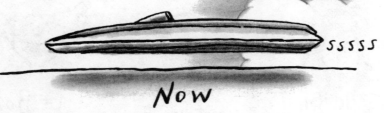

sssss

Now

60

Jet Trails

←to jet

1 min.

3 min.

5 min.

S

61

62 pendergast

Italian Arias

"Il Palazzo di Sophia"

"La Flatta"
(di Ferrari)

"Il gondolare
off Dutti"

"Il Papa, mi Papà"

"Il Pinchi
mi Culinni"
(Caro, Caro)

"Il Cinque Amendmentitti"

63

5. politics

65

BALLOT

CHOOSE One

☐ A Jerk from A major party

☐ A Nerd from the other

☐ A Nobody

pendergrast 67

68

U.S. IMAGE SINKS TO NEW LOWS

← Nato Ally
Spanish Olive
disdainfully
sticks out
pimento
at cocktail party

JP

69

DA -DA- <u>DUM</u> ! ! !

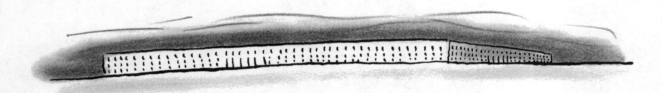

pendergrast

70

Communications

Then

Now

"I said,
'Friends,
Romans, and
Countrymen!'"

"10, 9,
8, ..."

MY
Fellow
Americans

pendergrast

71

I MARRIED a Politico...

pendergrast

72

6.

the

of

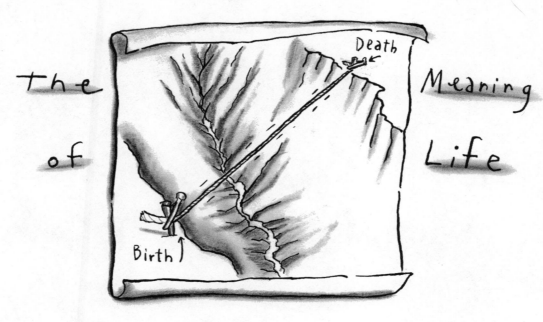

Meaning

Life

P

pendergrast

76

the Shoes of Life

P

Solitude

the Ideal

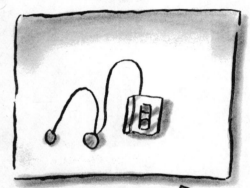

the Real Deal

pendergrast

Steppin' Out

the Honey Pot

Vinegar Time ← P.R. Problem

pendergrast

79

That's all she wrote

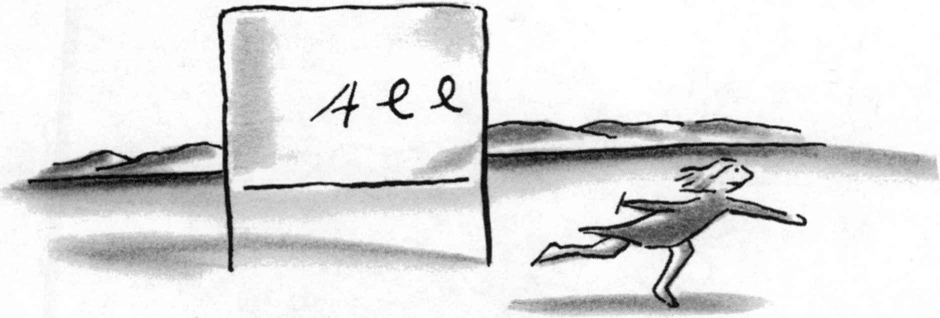

pendergrast

Hard
place

You are
Here

Rock

82   p e n d e r g r a s t

Overcome with Remorse, the Dallas Cowboys Cheerleaders enter a Convent

'YAY TEAM!'

CHARTER

pendergrast

83

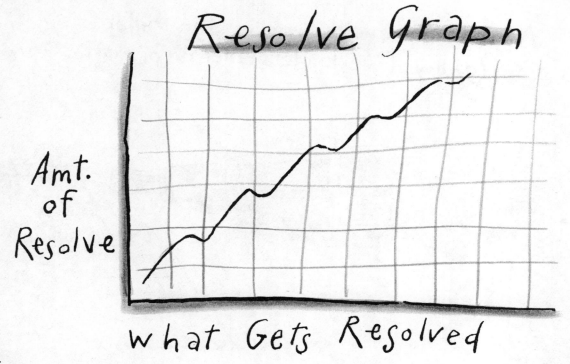

Resolve Graph

Amt.
of
Resolve

what Gets Resolved

84

ρ

7. Growing Up Normal

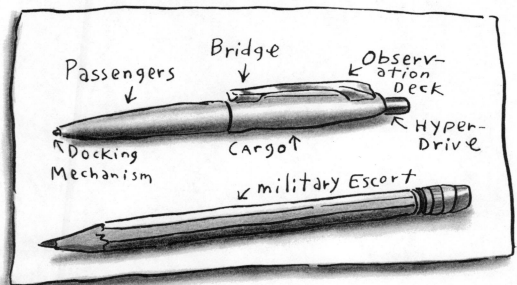

Passengers

Bridge

Observ-
ation
Deck

Docking
Mechanism

Cargo↑

Hyper-
Drive

←Military Escort

ß

Unsung heroes of the Old West

Pecos Donnie
Served Bravely in "the Battle of the Storm Drain" despite wet caps.

Patty Oakley
No matter how close the enemy, she always said, "You missed!" and ran away.

Hugh Boone
The best Indian Wrestler on Ash St.

P

I laughed

I cried

ᶜ

88

At Billy McCutchen's House...

Chimbly

B'sketti 'n'
Meat Balls

I try to find A dog-shaped spot on the wallpaper I HAd seen the DAY Before

90

One DAY while I was At SchooL...

sears Bill

Light Bill

Letter FRom my Grandmother saying my Dog, Lady, hAd Been Hit by A car.

pendergrast

91

Heaven

Hell

92

pendergrast

Day   Night

pendergrast

8. Love

(to ERR, Human)

97

we meet

My Book

Your Book

pendergrast

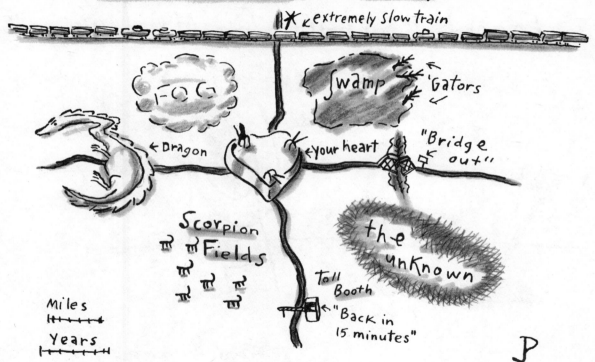

Treasure MAP

*← extremely slow train

FoG

Swamp

← 'Gators

← Dragon

← your heart

"Bridge out"

Scorpion Fields

the unknown

Toll Booth

"Back in 15 minutes"

Miles

Years

P

99

FOOLS
RUSH
In...

THE F...
acts

DANGER

pendergrast

101

Love Scales

←perfect moments

←pains in the ass

102

pendergrast

Love Chart

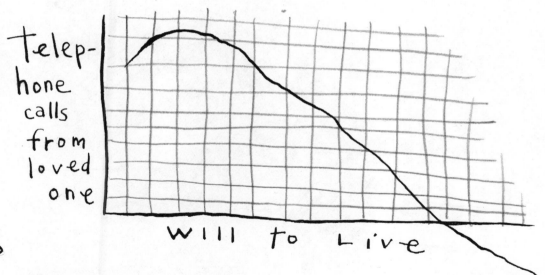

telep-
hone
calls
from
loved
one

will to Live

P

I Let Go

SAME
OLD
PLACE

Love 'n' Happiness

pendergrast

104

What's Left

Things to Do:
- Get Up
- Shower
- Work
- Dinner
- Pass Some Time
- Go to Bed
- ~~Dream~~
- etc.

106

pendergrast

Drowning Your Sorrows
(A Coward's Suicide)

Rum 'n' Cokes (y-axis): 0, 2, 4, 6, 8, 10

Urge to throw Up (x-axis): .3, .5, .8, 1.0, 1.3, 1.5 (etc.)

P 107

Awards 'n' Honors

NICE GUY

Medal

LAST PLACE

Ribbon

108

pendergrast

9. Snack Break

Flaubert's Twinkie

← Le plat

β

109

PLAT du Jour

pendergrast

La Nouvelle Cuisine

Porc Au Pine

112   pendergrast

Bar Chart

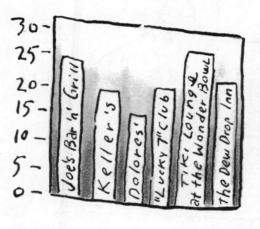

30 –
25 –
20 –
15 –
10 –
5 –
0 –

Joe's Bar 'n' Grill
Keller's
Dolores'
"Lucky 7" Club
Tiki Lounge at the Wonder Bowl
The Dew Drop Inn

P

Pie Chart

Pecan
Cherry
Lemon meringue
Choc.
Sweet 'tater
Apple
Punkin
Peach
← Rum Raisin

113

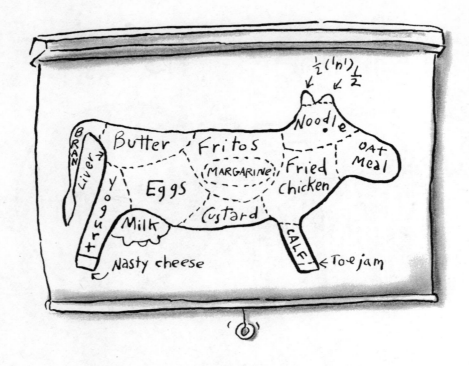

114

pendergrast

Bar Talk

Vodka Martini on
the rocks with
a lemon twist
(Vmart ↓∿)

Beefeater Gibson
straight Up
(Beef Gib↑)

p e n d e r g r a s t

115

La Nouvelle Cuisine

Rabbit with Trix Stuffing

116   pendergrast

10. The Further Adventures of Mike 'n' Spike

A Scratch
'n' sniff
Drawing

sniff

scratch

pendergrast

119

MiKe 'n' SPIKe
"Hey, MiKe, they're doin' 'Bohême' at the Met tonight"
OPERA
"SEEN it"

A Park Ave. Jaunt

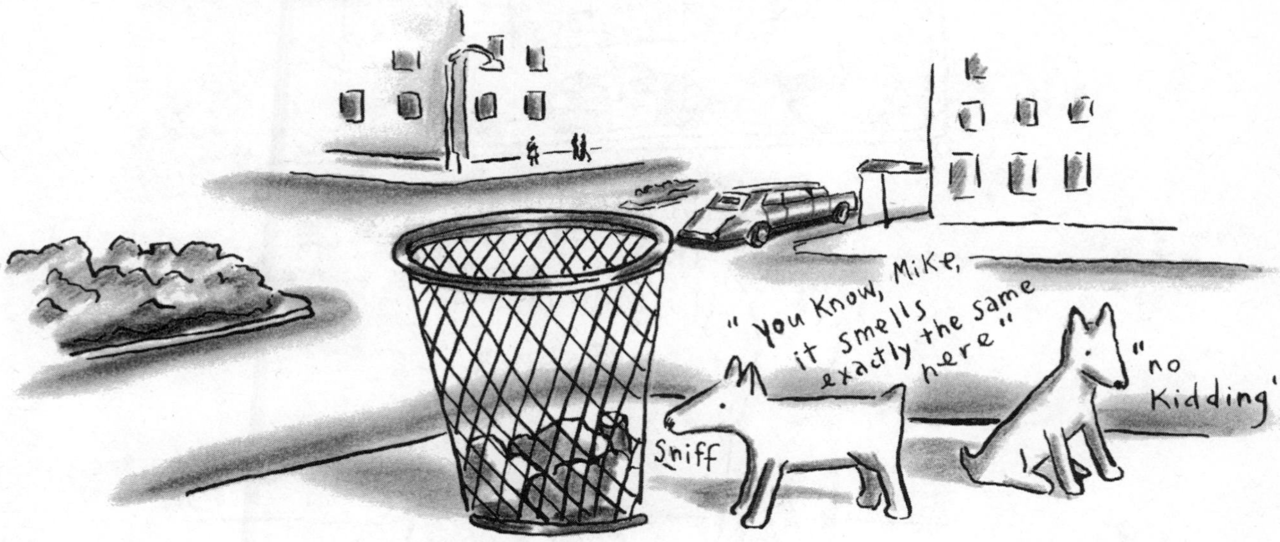

p e n d e r g r a s t

122 pendergrast

On the Town
Poodle Parlor
"C'mon, Mike, Don't Hog it, Man"
SNIFF
pendergrast

125

11.
The Devil's work-shop

The Devil's Remote Control

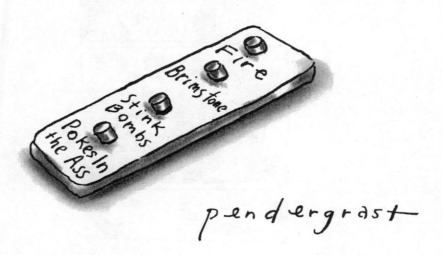

pendergrast

129

the Devil's Pantry

pendergrast

The Devil's Honor System

the Honor

the System

pendergnast

Stopping by Mr. D's for a Cocktail

Ice Cubes with "refrigerator smell"

Toenail clippings

pendergrast

134

12. "Objets D'Art"

"objets"

"D'Art"

P

135

← Art

← Gallery

ℐ

137

Gnu Descending a Staircase

pendergrast

IF YOU DON'T BUY
M E, I'M GOING TO JUMP

OFF THE BROOKLYN BRIDGE

SIGNED,
A DRAWING
P.S. I'M NOT KIDDING, BUSTER!

pendergrast

139

pendergrast

140

Nudie Sending A Staircase

POSTAGE

"Cleveland, please"

pendergrast 141

142

New D's Ending A Staircase

pendergrast

143

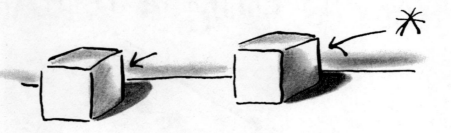

* etc.

pendergrast

life

pendergrast

145

Pillars of the Community

Dork

Ironic

Cornythian

pendergrast

Artist

History

St. Marks Gallery

Art

Life

Patron

pendergrast

147

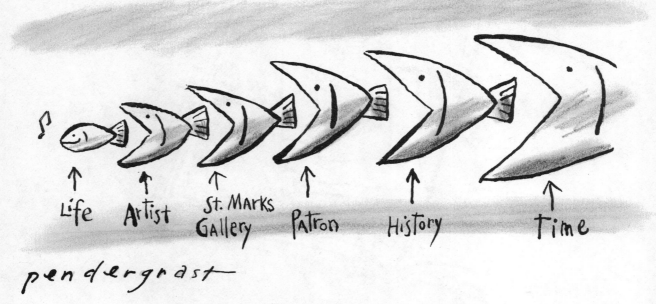

♪

↑   ↑   ↑   ↑   ↑   ↑
Life   Artist   St. Marks   Patron   History   time
                  Gallery

pendergast

148

Christo

Snack Bar

Ramses

"Art World"

pendergrast

149

‹ Drawing ›

pendergrast 85

150

13. A Peek into the Future

8

153

Computers will Have
our Emotions
for us

We regret
to inform
you your
canary

has died

pendergrast

154

FASHIONS OF THE FUTURE:

CAT NOSES

pendergrast

155

Terrorist

Artist

president

Druggie

ORDINA-RY PEOPle (of the 7UTURE)

pendergrast

156

pendergast

157

pendergrast

159